Somos una familia

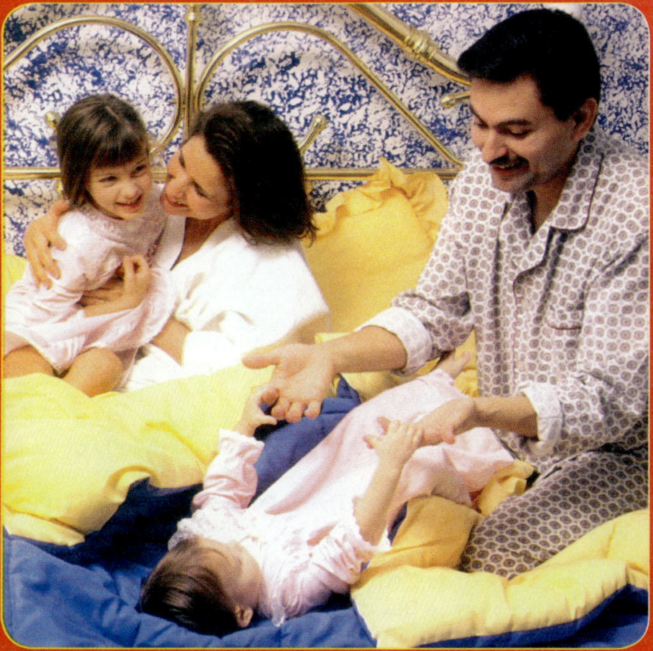

por Jeri Cipriano

Scott Foresman
is an imprint of

PEARSON

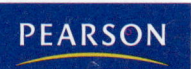

Glenview, Illinois • Boston, Massachusetts • Chandler, Arizona
Upper Saddle River, New Jersey

Every effort has been made to secure permission and provide appropriate credit for photographic material. The publisher deeply regrets any omission and pledges to correct errors called to its attention in subsequent editions.

Unless otherwise acknowledged, all photographs are the property of Pearson.

Photo locators denoted as follows: Top (T), Center (C), Bottom (B), Left (L), Right (R), Background (Bkgd)

Photographs **Opener** ©Stockbyte/Getty Images; **1** Bill Bachmann/Alamy Images; **3** ©UpperCut Images/SuperStock; **4** David Young-Wolff/PhotoEdit, Inc.; **5** ©PhotoAlto/SuperStock; **6** ©Kevin Laubacher/Getty Images; **7** ©Stockbyte/Getty Images; **8** Bill Bachmann/Alamy Images.

ISBN 13: 978-0-328-53299-5
ISBN 10:   0-328-53299-1

Copyright © by Pearson Education, Inc., or its affiliates. All rights reserved. Printed in the United States of America. This publication is protected by copyright, and permission should be obtained from the publisher prior to any prohibited reproduction, storage in a retrieval system, or transmission in any form or by any means, electronic, mechanical, photocopying, recording, or likewise. For information regarding permissions, write to Pearson Curriculum Rights & Permissions, One Lake Street, Upper Saddle River, New Jersey 07458.

Pearson® is a trademark, in the U.S. and/or other countries, of Pearson plc or its affiliates.

Scott Foresman® is a trademark, in the U.S. and/or other countries, of Pearson Education, Inc., or its affiliates.

2 3 4 5 6 7 8 9 10 V0N4 13 12 11 10

Somos una familia.
Mamá no puede cargar todo.
Ella quiere ayuda.

Somos una familia.
Luego guardamos todo bien.

Somos una familia.
Por la tarde jugamos.
¡Qué rico jugar con el balón!

Somos una familia.
Luego cenamos juntos.

Somos una familia.
Leemos buenos libros.
Nos gusta ver los dibujos.

"¡Somos una familia!", dijo mamá.
"Qué bien que estamos juntos".